Get Up

&

Walk

WHY SOME CHRISTIANS AREN'T HEALED

"All Glory Goes to God!"

Dontez D. Williams

Unless otherwise indicated scriptures are taken from the King James Version of the Bible.

Quotations marked NLT taken from:
Life Application Study Bible
New Living Translation
Copyright 2004
Tyndale House Publishers, Inc. | Wheaton, IL 60189

Published By:
MySheri Enterprises, LLC | Detroit, Michigan

Cover Design By: Sow Graphics & Publications, LLC | Detroit, Michigan
Editing By: Shairon Taylor, SLT Inspirations, LLC
Photography: Terrance Talton Photography

Dontez D. Williams
P.O. Box 141111
Detroit, Michigan 48214
www.savedbygracecm.com

ISBN: 978-0-9766782-4-3

TABLE OF CONTENTS

CHAPTER ONE

INTRODUCTION

... and a time to heal;
Ecclesiastes 3:3

Praise the Lord! The Lord woke me up at 4:30 one morning saying, "Get up and walk." I said to Him, "I'm not getting up and doing anything." Again, I heard God say in my spirit, "Get up and walk. This is why many people don't get their healing." He began to outline this whole book to me. By 6:30 that morning, I was halfway done. He began to show me through Scriptures why many people today don't get their healing.

I believe now more than ever that many people in the household of faith who are sick. The truth is there are too many Christians who are saved and sick. I believe the reason for this is because we have not activated our faith in the area of healing. Even though we know the right way, we have chosen a different path. It is important for us to regain our faith and grab a hold of healing now more than ever.

There are many things attached to salvation and healing is one of them. I believe the Lord wants to bring about a mighty move. The Lord wants our faith to be rekindled. The Lord gave me this book and I believe its contents will bless and bring about healing to a multitude of people.

God's word is never complicated. All you have to do is pay attention and listen to that still small voice inside. God wants to heal you. You must build up your faith and believe. If you don't believe healing is available, I pray that by the end of this book your faith will make you whole. I pray to the Father in Jesus' name that all who read this book will receive a revelation. I pray that healing comes to all who seek it. I pray also for all whose faith has been lost among sickness and disease. I also pray that God shows each person why they have not received their healing. After all these things I pray that you receive your healing.

Your healing is waiting within the pages of this book.

Thanks be to God for this revelation from him. May

God bless you and keep you.

CHAPTER TWO

YOUR SINS ARE FORGIVEN!

He said unto the sick of the palsy, "Son, thy sins be forgiven thee."

Mark 2:5

Get up and walk! Why is that such a hard thing for us to do? "Arise, take up your bed and walk." As Jesus preached to a full house, the Bible tells us of a man who is sick of the palsy being let down from the roof.

> *Mark 2:2-4 "And straightway many were gathered together, insomuch that there was no room to receive them, no, not so much as about the door: and he preached the word unto them. And they come unto him, bringing one sick of the palsy, which was borne of four. And when they could not come nigh unto him for the press, they uncovered the roof where he was: and when they had broken it up, they let down the bed wherein the sick of the palsy lay. When Jesus saw their faith, he said unto the sick of the palsy, Son, thy sins be forgiven thee."*

"Your sins are forgiven." That's a pretty odd

response to one who is sick, isn't it? This is such a hard thing for some of us to grasp. Your sins are forgiven! Many times, we stand before God praying for healing and God says, "You've been forgiven; now, forgive your brother." We may think, what does that have to do with my healing? We may wonder why God gives us these seemingly ridiculous commands. There's always criticism coming from other people. "Why haven't you been healed yet?" "Why has God left you out?" "What have you done to be sick?" "Where is your God now?"

Some of us haven't grasped the full concept of our faith. When we fully understand faith, we will see that there is healing available. Sometimes, we look at others and how they were healed. "Johnny sowed a seed and was healed" or "Pam had hands laid on her and was healed." Many times our sicknesses stem from the very sins that we have never asked forgiveness for. The forgiveness we hold back from others may be the cause of our sickness. We must be willing to be forgiven and must be willing to forgive.

> *Matthew 6:14-15 "For if ye forgive men their trespasses, your heavenly Father will also forgive you: But if ye forgive not men their trespasses, neither will your Father forgive your trespasses."*

Sometimes the reason we don't receive our healing is because we look at other people and think we should get it the same way. There are many ways to be healed. When we do pray for healing and God responds with, "your sins are forgiven," we say, "I know that, but I'm still sick." If you tell a sick person that their sins are forgiven, they might say, "I don't need to be forgiven; I need to be healed." Let's keep reading our text.

Mark 2:6-10 *But there were certain of the*

scribes sitting there, and reasoning in
their hearts, Why doth this man thus
speak blasphemies? Who can forgive sins
but God only? And immediately when
Jesus perceived in his spirit that they so
reasoned within themselves, He said unto
them, Why reason ye these things in your
hearts? Whether is it easier to say to the
sick of the palsy, Thy sins be forgiven
thee; or to say, Arise, and take up thy bed,
and walk?"

"What's easier?" This is the question He is asking some of us today, Which is easier? To say your sins are forgiven or take up your bed and walk? Many of us aren't willing to accept forgiveness and surely not ready to take up our beds and walk.

The scribes didn't realize it but an even greater miracle took place than the one they were expecting. This man's sins were forgiven. Jesus knew this sick man needed forgiveness. He also knew how he needed to be healed. The most important to Jesus was his sins to be forgiven. When we look at sickness and disease, we find that many of them are connected to sin. Whether it is the sin of the parents or the sin of the person, sickness is almost always connected to sin. They wanted him to walk; however, they didn't even realize the miracle that took place! The man's sins were still forgiven before he walked.

I feel in my spirit that God have told many of you how to grab onto your healing. God is working with many at this moment to bring about healing. God has spoken to some people and have showed them how to be healed and set free. However, they have not listened to His still small voice. There are some who need to simply let go of past sins so that they can walk in total healing. We can't get up and walk because we have an anchor of past sins. God wants us to lay aside our own guilt. Grab onto God's supernatural healing.

By His stripes you were healed.

> **1 Peter 2:24** *"Who his own self bare our sins in his own body on the tree, that we, being dead to sins, should live unto righteousness: by whose stripes ye were healed."*

Jesus is the one who will present you without spot on judgment day.

> **Revelation 7:14** *"And I said unto him, Sir, thou knowest. And he said to me, These are they which came out of great tribulation, and have washed their robes, and made them white in the blood of the Lamb.*

He holds nothing against you.

> **Isaiah 43:25** *"I, even I, am he that blotteth out thy transgressions for mine own sake, and will not remember thy sins."*

Now stop holding it against yourself!

This is what is so wonderful in this account of the paralyzed man. His sins were forgiven! Jesus died, rose again and your sins are already forgiven? As far as God is concerned, His grace is sufficient for you.

"And he said unto me, My grace is sufficient for thee: for my strength is made perfect in weakness. Most gladly therefore will I rather glory in my infirmities, that the power of Christ may rest upon me." **(2 Corinthians 12:9)**

Jesus could have just told the man to walk; however, he wanted to make sure that they knew He could forgive sins. See how our God operates? Your sins are forgiven, now get up and walk!

Notice how the man never complains? He didn't say, "Is that all?" He accepts that he may still have the palsy but he knows that his sins are forgiven. But many may feel that grace is not enough and that our healing more important. Then we don't accept our forgiveness and hence, we stay sick. Some don't fully understand the power of those stripes that were placed on Jesus. Since the foundation of the world, God promised to send Jesus to free us from sin.

> **Genesis 3:15** *"And I will put enmity between thee and the woman, and between thy seed and her seed; it shall bruise thy head, and thou shalt bruise his heel."*

We will continue to look at instances of healing and see how it was received. We will discuss why many people don't get healed. I pray that you grab onto your healing. The Bible teaches us that whatsoever we ask if we believe we can receive.

> *Mark 11:24 "Therefore I say unto you, What things soever ye desire, when ye pray, believe that ye receive them, and ye shall have them."*

It also teaches us there where two or three are gathered agreeing the Lord is present.

> *Matthew 18:20 "For where two or three are gathered together in my name, there am I in the midst of them."*

I am agreeing with you in prayer and declare you are the healed and not the sick. Now thank God for your healing!

Before we proceed, please say this prayer:

"Father, in the name of Jesus, I ask that you forgive me of my sins and heal my body. As I read this book, please open my eyes and spirit to hear anything I need to hear in order to embrace my healing. Father, I believe that Jesus died for my sins and I believe that He is your Son. Lord, I know that in the name of Jesus, I can be healed. Father, I'm believing you now for your healing power to come into my body and heal me. Thank you, Father, in the name of Jesus. I'm the healed and not the sick. Amen."

YOUR SINS ARE FORGIVEN!

YOUR SINS ARE FORGIVEN!

CHAPTER THREE

GO THY WAY: THY FAITH HAS MADE

YOU WHOLE!

Daughter, thy faith hath made thee whole; go
in peace, and be whole of thy plague
Mark 5:34

We learned that unforgiven sin is a reason some people don't receive their healing. Another reason many people don't receive their healing is because they don't have faith. They don't truly believe that they are healed, so they doubt. We like to say that whatsoever we ask, we receive. However, there is a prerequisite for that. We must believe in our hearts and doubt not. (Mark 11:24)

This is where many of us fall short. We don't fully believe in our hearts. We try to wait until it is too late. Then our faith is so little, we wonder why things don't happen, when all the time the same healing power is available now. The woman with the issue of blood knew she just had to touch him.

Mark 5:28 For she said, If I may touch but his clothes, I shall be whole.

She didn't have to wait until the pastor called

out her sickness. She knew that enough was enough and decided that Jesus was the only who could heal her. She was not going to be sick another day.

Isn't this how most of us is? We'll call the doctors or see the specialist; but seldom do we call on the name of Jesus—a name so powerful that one day every knee shall bow and confess He is Lord.

> **Romans 14:11 "For it is written, As I live, saith the Lord, every knee shall bow to me, and every tongue shall confess to God."**

That's all she needed. She didn't need a sermon. She didn't need hands laid on her. After she spent all she had and grew worse.

> *Mark 5:26 "And had suffered many things of many physicians, and had spent all that she had, and was nothing bettered, but rather grew worse."*

She needed a miracle. She didn't have time to wait in a healing line; she needed immediate healing, so she touched Jesus. When she had heard of Jesus, came in the press behind, and touched his garment.

Oh, but my God, the Lord can tell when you are tapping into his healing power.

> *Mark 5:27 & 30 "And Jesus, immediately knowing in himself that virtue had gone out of him, turned him about in the press, and said, Who touched my clothes?"*

Jesus can tell when you truly want to be healed. When you truly want to be healed, you won't wait until someone has to say it's your turn. You'll jump up and reach for your healing. You'll say a positive confession. You'll do all the things you promised yourself you would. You'll grab a hold to God's power and seize it. Your faith will make you whole!

> *Mark 5:34 "And he said unto her,*
> *Daughter, thy faith hath made thee*
> *whole; go in peace, and be whole of thy*
> *plague."*

The woman with the issue of blood was healed at the very moment she touched Jesus because she had faith she would be.

> *Mark 5:29 "And straightway the fountain*
> *of her blood was dried up; and she felt in*
> *her body that she was healed of that*
> *plague."*

Jesus knew He was touched and the person who touched Him was healed and had great faith. Jesus wanted to know who touched Him the others said, "Come on now a lot of people touched you."

> *Mark 5:30-31 "And Jesus, immediately*
> *knowing in himself that virtue had gone*
> *out of him, turned him about in the press,*
> *and said, Who touched my clothes? And*

his disciples said unto him, Thou seest the multitude thronging thee, and sayest thou, Who touched me?"

God looks for that one person with such great faith. He looks for that person who crawl because the pain is so severe. He looks for that woman who is full of shame and fear that she hides. Jesus knew that whoever touched Him came with expectancy. She came trembling, supposing she was in trouble; but His response to her story was "Go."

Mark 5:33 "But the woman fearing and trembling, knowing what was done in her, came and fell down before him, and told him all the truth."

He didn't want her to dwell on her last 12 years; no, He wanted her to go. He didn't need her to follow Him and testify. He wanted her to go on with her life.

That's what I hear Jesus saying now. "Go! Your

faith, has made you whole. Go in peace. Don't hold on to the past. Don't look up and down waiting for the right moment. Make the moment."

That woman was not in a line. She wasn't even the one Jesus was going to heal. Jesus was on His way to raise a little girl from the dead.

> *Mark 5:22-24 "And, behold, there cometh one of the rulers of the synagogue, Jairus by name; and when he saw him, he fell at his feet, And besought him greatly, saying, My little daughter lieth at the point of death: I pray thee, come and lay thy hands on her, that she may be healed; and she shall live. And Jesus went with him; and much people followed him, and thronged him."*

There was a multitude. Why didn't we read about anyone else touching Jesus and being healed? Because they already had their method of healing perceived in their head. For Jairus, the man whose daughter Jesus was going to heal, had his method of healing in mind. He believed that once Jesus laid hands on his daughter she would be healed. (Mark 5:23) His faith was rooted in the laying of Jesus' hands. The woman with the issue of blood knew that there might not be a chance for Jesus to lay hands on her. So she decided to lay hands on him. I can talk about that all day because it's such a wonderful story. She didn't have to be told where to receive her healing from she went and grabbed it. This is what the Lord wants you to do. Grab onto your healing. You have already been forgiven, now be healed!

When we finally get ready to be healed the power is there. The woman didn't have to wait until Jesus told her she was healed. The bible tells us at the very moment she touched him she was healed.

> **Mark 5:29 "And straightway the fountain of her blood was dried up; and she felt in her body that she was healed of that plague."**

We don't have to wait until the doctor says you are healed. You don't have to wait until you start feeling better. Start rejoicing now for your healing! Give the Lord a shout of praise! Give a victory shout and let the devil know that he is a liar. Let the devil know that you don't intend to be sick and Jesus has healed you. You are worthy to be healed. See, your sins have been forgiven if you have accepted the gift of salvation. You are glorious in God's eyes. Once you truly believe that in your heart, you shall be healed.

Sometimes we block our own healing with concepts of ourselves. We may think that we aren't worthy of healing. If Jesus healed the outcast known as a leper, He will surely heal you.

> *Matthew 8:2-3 "And, behold, there came a leper and worshipped him, saying, Lord, if thou wilt, thou canst make me clean. And Jesus put forth his hand, and touched him, saying, I will; be thou clean."*

Declare you are the healed, and not the sick. You are healed in Jesus' name. Lay hands on yourself and pray to the Father in Jesus' name. Grab onto His healing power, keep the faith and go in peace! Your faith will make you whole!

CHAPTER FOUR

WOULD YOU LIKE TO GET WELL?

When Jesus saw him and knew he had been ill for a long time, He asked him, Would you like to get well?
John 5:6 NLT

> *John 5:5 "And a certain man was there,*
> *which had an infirmity thirty and eight*
> *years."*

This man had been sick for 38 years. Jesus asked him, "Do you want to get well?" I love this story. The New Living Translation says the man said, *"I can't, sir for I have no one to put me into the pool when the water bubbles up. Someone else always gets there ahead of me."* **(John 5:7 NLT)** See what he tells Jesus? "I can't because there isn't anyone to help me." He just waited and waited.

Why didn't this man simply say yes? I feel this is another reason people do not grab onto their healing. They got comfortable with being sick and even arranged a lifestyle around it. For 38 years, he remained immobile. His only excuse was that someone else had to take him to the pool.

John 5:7 The impotent man answered him, Sir, I have no man, when the water is troubled, to put me into the pool: but while I am coming, another steppeth down before me

---

Many of us have excuses now. We talk about what we don't have or can't get. But what was Jesus' response? *"Rise, take up thy bed, and walk!"* (John 5:8) Jesus didn't say, "Well. look I'll help you get into the pool." He simply told him to get up. This is a great story.

This man was more than prepared to be an invalid because he was programmed to be one. This man could have lived another 20 years with the excuse that someone else couldn't help him to the pool. Many of us have excuses as to why we haven't received healing or deliverance. For example, "I can't stop smoking because I get nervous." All Jesus is asking is, "Do you want to be healed?"

Why didn't Jesus just say, "be healed"? Why did He ask that question to a man who was near to the same healing source as others? Wasn't it obvious that he wanted to be healed? There are many in churches today who will pray and lay hands on others and yet they remain sick themselves. When it's their time to be healed they'll be healed they feel. Once again, Jesus is asking, "Do you want to be healed?" If you do want to be healed, "Get up and walk."

Over a decade ago, I found myself being tired and I had lost a lot of weight. I knew that the doctor said I had a thyroid problem but I never sought medical attention because I lost my insurance. See my excuse? During the same time, my goddaughter's mother was in the hospital. She was near death and we went and laid hands on her. She got well and a year later, I'm still feeling terrible. Every day, I got even more tired. I didn't feel like getting out of the bed. I would eat and eat but couldn't seem to pick up any weight.

Finally, I made a doctor's appointment. I knew I'd have to pay out of pocket but I didn't want to take any chances. I went to my appointment and the doctor said "hyperthyroidism." Basically, my thyroid was overworking and that was causing me to feel tired and lose weight. He wanted me to take some tests to see what the full extent of my disorder was. I figured I'd get billed but to my dismay, I had to pay $1,000 upfront. Now, if that doesn't activate faith, I don't know what will. I didn't have that type of money to take a test at that time. So, I got serious and prayed. I began to tap into God's healing power and battled the devil and his lies and propaganda. I heard the Lord ask, "Do you want to be healed? Look to me." My answer was, "Yes, I want to be healed."

One day, the Spirit of the Lord told me I was healed. That word changed my life. I know that I was healed. I picked up some weight and my energy level is great. Thanks be to God!

See what happened? I didn't fully believe God's healing was available to me although I had seen someone who was near death be healed. In fact, she began to improve the next day after I prayed and laid hands on her.

I was going to a great church with an anointed healing ministry, but I got used to being tired. I'd make excuses for myself like, "I stayed up late," "I need a new pillow," and "I need another bed." The truth was, I refused to truly activate my faith by getting up and doing something about it. Many times we don't even accept the fact that we are sick and therefore, we can't be healed. I saw the weight drop. I felt the fatigue. Yet, I still didn't want to believe I was sick. Did that stop me from being sick? No! So ask yourself, "Do I want to be well?" Do I want God's healing in my body?" He'll say to you like He said to me, "you're healed." When you are truly ready to be healed, God will heal you. You have to be ready to "take up your bed" of excuses. "Walk" away from the comfort zone of your disability or sickness. Stand up and tell the devil that by Jesus' stripes, you are healed. The blood of Jesus has brought about miraculous healing in your body.

The testimony of my personal healing doesn't stop there. When I finally got my health insurance back I visited the doctor to check the thyroid out. The doctor came back with the test results and said, "there's nothing wrong with your thyroid!" Glory to God! When I tell you God is a healer, it's because He healed me!

Another reason many people may have lost the healing power they once received is due to sin. This is takes us to the next chapter, "Stop Sinning."

CHAPTER FIVE

STOP SINNING

… now you are well; so stop sinning, or something
even worse may happen to you.
John 5:14 NLT

This is another reason many people receive healing for only a short amount of time and some even become worse. They continue to live sin-filled lives. They continue to fornicate. They continue to walk in death. The Lord says He "sets in front of you life and death... choose life." (Deuteronomy 30:19) God doesn't stop us from choosing death.

How many people do we know who go to church, have hands laid on them and the next day is at a club? Many people are oppressed by demons. Sometimes these demons are rebuked and cast out of the body. However, Scripture tell us that when a demon leaves the body he comes back with seven demons more powerful than himself.

Matthew 12:45 "Then goeth he, and taketh with himself seven other spirits more wicked than himself, and they enter in and dwell there: and the last state of that man is worse than the first. Even so shall it be also unto this wicked generation."

He is determined to get back into the body.

Luke 11:24-26 "When the unclean spirit is gone out of a man, he walketh through dry places, seeking rest; and finding none, he saith, I will return unto my house whence I came out. And when he cometh, he findeth it swept and garnished. Then goeth he, and taketh to him seven other spirits more wicked than himself; and they enter in, and dwell there: and the last state of that man is worse than the first."

The devil never intends to leave you alone. This is why you must not give the devil a place.

Ephesians 4:27 "Neither give place to the devil."

The devil loves nothing more than a sad or sick Christian. He wants you to keep on sinning. This way, he can send his demons back into your life. We need to do a little "inner" house cleaning. We need to make sure that once we have grabbed a hold of God's healing we stop sinning and if we do sin we make sure we get forgiveness.

> *1 John 1:9 "If we confess our sins, he is faithful and just to forgive us our sins, and to cleanse us from all unrighteousness."*

Jesus gave him the option of life or death. Jesus is saying to many of us today, "Choose life." The more knowledge you have, the more responsibility you acquire. You are responsible for doing the things which you have been taught.

> *(Luke 12:48) "But he that knew not, and did commit things worthy of stripes,*

shall be beaten with few stripes. For unto whomsoever much is given, of him shall be much required: and to whom men have committed much, of him they will ask the more."

A lot of people get healed and go on living their lives as though they were never sick. Some even stop going to church, stop praying and/or stop reading their Bible. They continue to do all the things of this world, not realizing that they are putting themselves in jeopardy. They stop praising the Lord and get upset when something worse comes on them. This is not God's doing; it is their fault. The Bible is replete with commands from God. The Bible teaches us how to live. God has given us pastors and teachers, which are part of the five-fold ministry. Pastors and teachers labor to bring each individual God has assigned to them to maturity.

Ephesians 4:11 "And he gave some, apostles; and some, prophets; and some, evangelists; and some, pastors and teachers;"

The Lord has equipped us with knowledge so we will not perish.

Hosea 4:6 "My people are destroyed for lack of knowledge: because thou hast rejected knowledge, I will also reject thee, that thou shalt be no priest to me: seeing thou hast forgotten the law of thy God, I will also forget thy children."

I found something very interesting during my studies. Genesis 2:17 says, *"But of the tree of knowledge of good and evil thou shalt not eat of it: for in the day thou eatest thereof thou shalt surely die."* What the Scripture is saying that in "dying you will die." The sin caused the sicknesses that man would later die from. Adam and Eve began to age and decay the moment they ate of the fruit. The devil knows that our sins will kill us. He tries to convince us that they won't. He'll tell us that God isn't going to do anything. To a certain extent, he is right. God has set laws and everything operates according to the laws. When we break the laws, we hurt ourselves. The devil tries to convince us that we misunderstood. He told Eve that she wouldn't die right then. He was right; but in dying, she surely died. Adam released into this world not only sin, but death by sin.

Romans 5:19 *"For as by one man's disobedience many were made sinners, so by the obedience of one shall many be made righteous."*

The paralyzed man at the pool had to choose either life and death. Today is the day for you to make a choice. Today is also the day for you to receive and thank God for your healing and sin no more. Turn your life over to him. Stop sinning because sin brings about death.

Romans 6:23 "For the wages of sin is death; but the gift of God is eternal life through Jesus Christ our Lord."

If you already live your life for God, hallelujah! Keep doing that which is right. If you haven't received your healing, say this prayer: Father, Jehovah, the one who reveals, in the name of Jesus, I pray that you reveal to me where I have fallen short. I pray that you'll forgive me of any sins I have committed. If I have anything against anyone, I forgive them. Father, I know that by Jesus' stripes, I was healed. Therefore, I declare that I'm the healed and not the sick. I proclaim a new life in Christ and I thank you for the healing. Amen.

Continue to thank God for His healing. Give praises to Him for His words are powerful!

STOP SINNING

STOP SINNING

CHAPTER SIX

SPEAK THE WORD ONLY

The centurion answered and said, ...but speak the word only,
and my servant shall be healed.

Matthew 8:8

When I first found out about my thyroid, I told my spiritual father and he said, "Don't tell anyone else you are sick and as I'm talking to you, I'm rebuking it in the name of Jesus." Why did he do this? Why did he tell me not to tell anyone I was sick when I was? He didn't want me to spread the lies of the devil. Instead, I should have been confessing the Word of God over my situation. I was the redeemed of the Lord and I needed to say so.

> *Psalm 107:2 Let the redeemed of the*
> *LORD say so, whom he hath redeemed*
> *from the hand of the enemy;*

He didn't want me to tell a lot of people who would in turn tell others. We needed more positive confessions than negative ones.

I couldn't allow my situation to determine my life. I couldn't accept the lies of the devil. Instead, I had to find what the Word of God said about my situation. I had to confess that faith comes by hearing and that I would hear only from the Word of God.

> *Romans 4:17 (As it is written, I have made thee a father of many nations,) before him whom he believed, even God, who quickeneth the dead, and calleth those things which be not as though they were.*

I began to declare that I was the healed and not the sick. I would say to myself that by Jesus' stripes, I was healed.

> *1 Peter 2:24 Who his own self bare our sins in his own body on the tree, that we, being dead to sins, should live unto righteousness: by whose stripes ye were healed.*

I laid hands on myself. I prayed in the spirit, gave thanks and made my requests known before God.

> *Philippians 4:6 Be careful for nothing; but*

in every thing by prayer and supplication
with thanksgiving let your requests be
made known unto God.

I knew I had a great calling on my life. If I gave into the devil's lies, I never would have been able to fulfill that calling. As I began to confess the word and speak that word only, a great turnaround occurred. The Lord gave me a word regarding my situation. After I prayed and waited, this is what the Lord placed in my spirit:

"Truth is higher than fact. The fact may be that the doctor says something is wrong; but the truth is that I say you are healed in Jesus' name. Thus saith God, through the spirit of grace. Keep up your head and countenance of face. Never before has there been an attack but in all things you will not lack. Though the doctor says something is wrong it won't be for too long. Just keep faith and do not give in. For you suffer but not for sin. You suffer for only a while. So that even the devil will smile. Then as he is ready to laugh it will be over at last. For I the Lord do say to you the facts may be, but I have truth. For do not say you are sick for from this day I call you healed. And in a little while it will all be revealed. Thus, saith the Lord and the spirit of grace; smile don't let a frown be on your face. For I the Lord has healed you hear the facts but know the truth."

After I wrote that down and read it, tears came. "I suffer, but not for sin." I began living a righteous, holy life. I was going to a wonderful Word teaching church I was tithing and seeking the kingdom. So, I wondered, why now? Why did I have to be sick at such a time in my life when I was living holy? The devil wanted me to believe I was being punished when in fact, had been redeemed. When that word of the Lord came, I rejoiced and three days later, I knew I was healed. When someone asks me if I still have that thyroid problem, I tell them no because I truly believe that it's gone. I don't have any of the symptoms that I had before. I thank God for that every day.

Speaking the word is powerful! Many are familiar with the story in the Bible of the centurion who had a servant who was sick with the palsy. He asked Jesus to heal him and Jesus tells him that He will come and heal him.

> *Matthew 8:8-10 "The centurion answered and said, Lord, I am not worthy that thou shouldest come under my roof: but speak the word only, and my servant shall be healed. For I am a man under authority having soldiers under me: and I say to this man, Go, and he goeth; and to another, Come, and he cometh; and to my servant, Do this, and he doeth it. When Jesus heard it, he marveled, and said to*

them that followed, Verily I say unto you,
I have not found so great faith, no, not in
Israel."

The centurion knew that there was power in the word. Proverbs also tells us that there is life and death in the tongue.

Proverbs 18:21 Death and life are in the power of the tongue: and they that love it shall eat the fruit thereof.

The centurion knew that his servant was near death. He felt unworthy having Jesus even set foot in his house. "Just speak the word. Just say my servant is healed and I believe it will be done." See that faith? That is amazing faith. Jesus Himself said that He hasn't seen such great faith, not in Israel. Why can't we do the same? Why don't we speak the word over our situations? Why do we constantly let the devil lie to us and tell us we are sick? When we can speak the word only? We should tell the devil he is a liar. We have been healed and it's time we start acting like it. Take your life back!

What was Jesus' response to the centurion? Did you expect a sermon? Or a reassurance that He had to be there to witness the miracle? Did we expect Jesus to tell the man that he insists and to go despite the man's request? Instead Jesus simply says, ***"Go thy way; and as thou has believed, so be it done unto thee." And this servant was healed in the selfsame hour.*** (Matthew 8:13)

The first thing He tells him is to go his way. Then He tells him as he believed, so be it—as he believed, not as Jesus believed. Jesus knew that this man's faith wasn't conditioned on what he saw. The centurion didn't need Jesus to be there physically to get his servant healed. "Speak the word only" was his request.

Nowadays, many of us feel as though we need a whole infantry of evangelists and pastors to lay hands on us. Meanwhile, all we have to do is "speak the word." Isn't that such an amazing story? "As you believe so it is done to thee." God has many ways of healing, but you must believe.

Where's your faith? Is it based on what you see? Do you have to see it like Thomas in order to believe it?

> *John 20:24-25 But Thomas, one of the twelve, called Didymus, was not with them when Jesus came. The other disciples therefore said unto him, We have seen the LORD. But he said unto them, Except I shall see in his hands the print of the nails, and put my finger into the print of the nails, and thrust my hand into his side, I will not believe.*

Are you comfortable believing God for your

healing even though you still feel sick? Are you willing to confess that you are the healed and not the sick? Do you believe that healing is still available? Do you know that the Lord loves you and wants you well? Remember what He asked the man at the pool: "Do you want to be well?" The choice is up to you. You must speak the word only and believe, and you will be healed.

Many of us are still sick because instead of declaring we are healed, we say, "Woe is me." We feed into that lie. We buy the lie from the devil and lend it to others. Then we get mad at God because we haven't been healed. But as Jesus said, "As thou believed so be it done unto thee." If you believe you are going to be sick, chances are you will be. If you believe that you will be well, you will be. God doesn't change. If He healed that centurion's servant based on his faith, what more will He do for you?

There are many who have prayed for family and friends. Some may have prayed and then a day later, they confessed that the person was still sick. We must stop doing this. We can't keep praying to God asking for healing while declaring we are sick. We must believe that we are well.

This is what I had to do with my goddaughter's mother. Anytime I heard someone say she was sick, I would immediately correct them and say, "She was sick but she has been healed." As she grew worse, I would say, "She is getting better." As she was transferred from the hospital to the nursing home, I would confess that she was healed. Remember we prayed and believed that she would recover. The Lord let me know that she would be healed. Therefore, I just had to be patient. Her temperature would rise, her heart rate would be dangerously high and her blood pressure dangerously low and I would confess that she was healed. Whenever she told me that she was getting worse, I would tell her, "It's only the devil, now stop saying that." I was speaking the word only and believing. I would not allow myself or anyone else to bring about negative results. After all, she did have a baby to raise. Now, she is as healthy as a horse and I thank God for that. Through her experience, I was able to see God's healing power! Thanks be to God, great things He has done! Hallelujah!

CHAPTER SEVEN

DO I LIKE BEING SICK?

And a certain man lame from his mother's womb was
carried... to ask alms of them that entered into the temple.

Acts 3:2

I know some people are thinking, "What is he I thinking? Do I like being sick? Who would like to be sick? What good things come to those who are sick?" It's not too uncommon for us to hear of a parent who revels in the attention of a sick child. I know people who revel in attention from their own sickness. It's almost as if their sickness is a crutch used to hold up their life. They use their sickness to get sympathy from others.

We find that the man at the gate called Beautiful in Acts 3 who used his disability as a means of collecting money.

> *Acts 3:2 And a certain man lame from his mother's womb was carried, whom they laid daily at the gate of the temple which is called Beautiful, to ask alms of them that entered into the temple;*

This man was carried daily to the temple to beg.

This is how many of us are today. We get so used to being sick, that we begin to fully accept it. We begin to accept that we won't be able to have children. We accept the fact that our mother or father had cancer, so we will probably have it, too. We accept the doctor's diagnosis that we have diabetes. We accept the heart attack that we are bound to have due to genetics. We accept the fact that a stroke is imminent. We accept being laid at a gate daily to beg from those who have decided not to let unfortunate situations determine their life.

Acts 3:3 Who seeing Peter and John about to go into the temple asked an alms.

Many times, we see a man of God and ask them for things we don't need. We may say, "If I only had the money, I wouldn't be sick." This man at the gate received money every day and still was sick. Notice

Peter's response after the lame asked an alms.

> *And Peter, fastening his eyes upon him*
> *with John, said, Look on us. (Acts 3:4)*

Peter wanted the man to look at them. This is what I hear Jesus saying, "Look to the cross." Look to the cross, for it is on that you were healed. *"And he gave heed unto them, expecting to receive something of them."* (Acts 3:5) The man still didn't understand what was happening. He looked at them expecting to receive alms. Many of us in the church are doing the same thing. We come expecting something different from what we get. We hear the pastor talk about how to receive healing and then get mad because he doesn't hold a healing line. We get mad when I can almost hear him say, "Look at what I said." The man wasn't thinking about getting well. He probably didn't know it was available or didn't believe it was available. All he wanted from them was a handout.

Many people only want a handout. We want to get through on others faith. We don't want to activate our own faith. We become used to being laid at our own gates and consider them Beautiful. We get used to being the poor lame person physically and/or spiritually. We need to ask ourselves, "Do I like being sick?"

> *Then Peter said, Silver and gold have I none but such as I have give I thee: in the name of Jesus Christ of Nazareth rise up and walk. (Acts 3:6)*

Many of us expect silver and gold when all the time all we have to do is rise up. Notice the man had to do something. He had to rise up. Rise up out of his situation. Rise up and tap into the healing power of Christ. *And he took him by the right hand, and lifted him up: and immediately his feet and ankle bones received strength.* **(Acts 3:7)** God will lift you up if you are willing to stand. When he released his faith, he received strength. I hear the Lord saying, "I've tried to give you strength but you haven't activated your faith." Let's see what else this man did once he activated his faith.

> *Acts 3:8-9 And he leaping up stood, and walked, and entered with them into the temple, walking and leaping, and praising God. And all the people saw him walking and praising God.*

He leaped up, stood and walked. He picked up his bed and walked. Are we really willing to rise up and walk? How many of us are willing to leave our gates where we once were laid? Are we ready to leave our comfort zones? Once you decide that enough is enough, you will tap into that healing power of God and others will see you praising God. They will wonder, "Is that the same person who once couldn't walk because of arthritis?" "Isn't that the person who couldn't breathe because of asthma?" The Lord is ready and able to heal you, but you first must decide you are ready. When you're ready to be healed, rejoice like you're healed. You will see manifestations. In fact, you will see it once you believe it. John 11:40 (NIV) says, *Then Jesus said, "Did I not tell you that if you believe, you will see the glory of God?"*

So ask yourself, "Do I like to be sick?" Chances are you don't. Then you will be like the man in Acts 3. You'll get up, leaping and praising God because He will heal you.

So jump up and give the Lord a shout of praise! Don't become dependent on dependencies. Don't get used to your situations because you have healing available to you. You are the healed and not the sick.

Now is the time to act like you are healed. Rejoice and give thanks for your healing!

CHAPTER EIGHT

BE THANKFUL!

And Jesus answering said, "Were there not ten cleansed? But where are the nine?"

Luke 17:17

Luke 17:11-19 And it came to pass, as he went to Jerusalem, that he passed through the midst of Samaria and Galilee. And as he entered into a certain village, there met him ten men that were lepers, which stood afar off: And they lifted up their voices, and said, Jesus, Master, have mercy on us. And when he saw them, he said unto them, Go show yourselves unto the priests. And it came to pass, that, as they went, they were cleansed. And one of them, when he saw that he was healed, turned back, and with a loud voice glorified God, and fell down on his face at his feet, giving him thanks: and he was a Samaritan. And Jesus answering said, were there not ten cleansed? But where are the nine? There are not found that returned to give glory to God, save this stranger. And he said unto him, Arise, go thy way: thy faith hath made thee whole.

This account in Luke 17 is very important for us

to understand. There were ten lepers who were cleansed. We find that only one came and gave God the glory. Jesus commented on this man for doing such. Think about how many people you know who get something from God and forget they even knew Him. How many people get something from another person and forget all about that person? I believe that this is another reason people can't keep their healing. They forget about God. They pray to God and get healed and then all the glory goes to the doctors. Let's understand something: To be cleansed doesn't necessarily mean that you will remain that way.

I made a big deal out of this with my goddaughter's mother. I wanted her to know that no matter what the doctors did to help her, all the glory goes to God. I wanted her to know that once the surgery was successful, it was God who navigated the doctors' hands. It was God who gave them the knowledge. Many times, we get our healing and we don't go back to God to give Him the glory.

Jesus asked the one where were the other nine. He wanted to know why they didn't come back to give God the glory. He doesn't tell them that they will be healed. He only tells them to go show themselves to the priest. By Jewish law, the priest was the only person to determine if a person was free of leprosy. As they traveled to the priest, all ten were cleansed. Many times, many people are healed at one time. That's why it isn't so uncommon for ten people to have the same illness and there be ten different results. The man knew that this miracle was only the work of God and wanted to give God the glory. He didn't wait until he went to the priest. He knew that he was healed. He went back to Jesus.

"Arise, go thy way, your faith has made you whole." Again Jesus commands him to "arise." He wanted the man to get off his knees and go. Then he tells him to "Go thy way: your faith has made you whole."

It was his faith. He was already cleansed. What did he mean by saying he was whole? His sins were forgiven. He would never have that plague again. When the Lord heals you, you are truly healed.

> *Jeremiah 17:14 Heal me, O LORD, and I shall be healed; save me, and I shall be saved: for thou art my praise.*

When we truly receive our healing, we won't have to worry about being sick again. When Jesus heals you, there will be no need for medicine. You will be made whole. The Lord is more than able to heal. We just have to put ourselves in position to be healed. We have to make sure we are willing to be healed. We must believe that we can be healed. This is important and it's

our next chapter.

CHAPTER NINE

DO YOU BELIEVE YOU CAN BE HEALED?

And so he did only a few miracles there because of their unbelief.

Matthew 13:58 NLT

The biggest reason people can't receive their healing is because they don't believe in healing. You would be surprised at how many people read the Bible and all the accounts of healing, and yet don't believe that healing is available now. Some may say, "That was then, but this is now."

Throughout this book, we have seen that faith plays a key role in the healing of a person. Almost all cases involved the faith of the person who needed the healing. How can you receive something you don't believe it?

]Some may believe that healing is available but don't believe that they are supposed to be healed. Jesus encountered this with the people in His day. They did not believe in what Jesus was saying simply because they knew Him since he was little.

Matthew 13:53-58 And it came to pass, that when Jesus had finished these parables, he departed thence. And when

he was come into his own country, he

taught them in their synagogue, insomuch

that they were astonished, and said,

Whence hath this man this wisdom, and

these mighty works? Is not this the

carpenter's son? is not his mother called

Mary? and his brethren, James, and Joses,

and Simon, and Judas? And his sisters,

are they not all with us? Whence then

hath this man all these things? And they

were offended in him. But Jesus said unto

them, A prophet is not without honour,

save in his own country, and in his own

house. And he did not many mighty

works there because of their unbelief.

This is what many of us do. We don't believe

that we can have hands laid on us and be healed

because the one laying hands is a person just like us.

We don't see past the person and see the anointing that

rests on that person.

Jesus was unable to do great miracles like he was able to do in other countries. " He said that, *"A prophet is not without honor save his own country and in his own house."* (Matthew 13:57) This is the same with many of us today. We won't let a relative lay hands on us because they came from the same place we came from. I've heard some say that there isn't a such thing as receiving the Holy Ghost and falling out under the power of God. Unbelief is the reason the Gentiles have been given a chance to enter into the Kingdom.

> *Romans 11:20 Well; because of unbelief they were broken off, and thou standest by faith. Be not highminded, but fear:*

Unbelief keeps many of us from receiving our healing. You must go to the Word of God to build up your faith. You need to find out what the Bible says about your situations. You have to believe what the Word of God says. Read the accounts of healing in the

Bible. Get to a Word-teaching church. Get out of your comfort zone.

I hear the Lord saying, "Arise." Don't be scared to move. "Go thy way!" Stop making excuses. Stop feeling sorry for yourself. Once you have built up your faith, you will see how greatly God will move in your life.

Remember the boy who was vexed with an evil spirit that violently seized him?

Mark 9:17-18 (NLT) One of the men in the crowd spoke up and said, "Teacher, I brought my son so you could heal him. He is possessed by an evil spirit that won't let him talk. And whenever this spirit seizes him, it throws him violently to the ground. Then he foams at the mouth and grinds his teeth and becomes rigid.

Notice what happens next.

Mark 9:18-19 (NLT) So I asked your

> *disciples to cast out the evil spirit, but*
> *they couldn't do it. Jesus said to them,*
> *"You faithless people! How long must I*
> *be with you? How long must I put up*
> *with you? Bring the boy to me.*

Jesus called the people faithless. They didn't believe the demon could be cast out, so they brought the boy. But when the evil spirit saw Jesus, it threw the child into a violent convulsion, and he fell to the ground, writhing and foaming at the mouth. "How long has this been happening?" Jesus asked the boy's father.

He replied, "Since he was a little boy. The spirit often throws him into the fire or into water, trying to kill him. Have mercy on us and help us, if you can. (Mark 9:20-22 NLT) *The boy's father said, "Help us if you can."* He honestly didn't fully believe in what he was asking for. Notice what Jesus says.

Mark 9:23-24 (NLT) "What do you mean,
If I can? "Anything is possible if a person
believes." The father instantly cried out,
"I do believe, but help me overcome my
unbelief."

Anything is possible if a person believes. Such a beautiful thought and how true it is. That is why it is so important to ask yourself if you truly believe you can be healed. If you have a problem with unbelief, ask God to help you overcome it. You might say or think, "I do believe, but every time I get a little better, I feel worse." You might even say, "As soon as I get better, the symptoms come back. What do I do?" You have to keep confessing the Word of God.

Remember, speak the word only! Don't let yourself become of victim of the devil's propaganda. Stop sinning and give your life to God. The devil is very happy to make you think that you are sick. You have a greater covenant in Christ Jesus.

You are a new creature in Christ and something new shouldn't be sick or broke! Jesus has already taken away your sins and He has healed you. Jesus has set up trust fund in all our names. It is not His fault if we don't claim our inheritance and seize the things set up for us. Believe me, healing is in the trust fund. Go and claim your inheritance! So rejoice and be glad! Thank God for your healing. It's never complicated. Many times we hold back our own healing. We stop the blessing. Stop holding yourself back from your blessing. Anything is possible if a person believes. So get up and walk! Go get your healing!

CHAPTER TEN

PRACTICAL TIPS ON HEALING

I could not end this book without sharing some practical wisdom. As I was reflecting on this book with my editor, Elder Shairon Parks, one of the things I noticed was that some think that just because they are sick, they do not have faith. You must understand that just because you, as a child of God, do not get healed does not mean that you do not have faith. In fact, some of you will read this book and discover that your healing is near to you. As a child of God, we must understand the importance of our bodies being the temple of the Holy Spirit. Think about that for a minute. The Holy Spirit dwells in your body! What type of environment is your body for the Holy Spirit?

The Lord began to convict me about things that I should be doing to better protect my temple. There are things that we do that is detrimental to our health and wellness. Some of you are smoking, drinking in excess, not exercising, not drinking enough water or drinking too much pop/soda, etc. We must become intentional with our healing and understand that God is looking for us to keep our temples protected. If there was an app that the Holy Spirit was able to use to review His stay in your body, what would His review be of the environment? Would the Holy Spirit give you a five-star rating? I do not present myself as a health expert, but there are some things that I desire to share that I pray will be beneficial to you.

1. **Drink plenty of water.** This is so practical and yet many of us have a hard time getting the eight glasses of water we need each day. Your body needs water to survive. You would be surprised at the ailments that could easily be reversed if you simply had enough water in your body. I usually keep a glass or bottle next to my bed to drink as soon as I wake up. I may even

drink between two or three glasses before I leave the house in the morning. Water is vital; make a decision to stay hydrated.

2. **Get plenty of rest.** When I was younger, my grandma would tell me to rest. I would respond by saying that there was plenty of time to rest when you are dead. When I reflect on that statement, I realize how asinine it was. Resting is not a privilege; it is a need. Even Jesus rested. In fact, God rested. This lets us know that it is important for us to rest. Think about this: God created man on the sixth day and the next day was a day of rest. I believe that God did that to teach man the importance of rest. Jesus often took that needed time away from His disciples and the multitudes to get by Himself in order to refuel, recharge and to rest.

3. **Exercise at least 30 minutes a day**. I've learned that

this is a great way to stay healthy. Just 30 minutes a day can really make a difference in your life. I like to go to the gym and ride the elliptical. The elliptical is relaxing; it allows me to burn off steam and focus on my body. Some people enjoy taking walks, riding bikes or running. Whatever activity you choose, stay consistent with it. Studies have shown that just 30 minutes of exercise can reduce your blood pressure and other health risks.

4. **Take your vitamins.** Many people have vitamin deficiencies. I believe that many of those who are on prescription medication can have their health issues resolved simply by taking vitamins. For example, my wife has low iron. She cannot take the iron pills because she experiences bad side effects. However, she takes Blood Builder vitamins from the health food store or Blackstrap Molasses which works wonders for her iron

levels. When she is consistent with taking her vitamins, she has no symptoms. Glory to God!

5. Seek healthy alternatives and natural remedies. It is no secret that there is a "Balm in Gilead." I believe God has given us herbs and plants that can heal any ailment. I encourage you to seek more homeopathic alternatives to medicine. Now, I am not saying don't take medicine—I encourage you to use wisdom. Living here in Michigan, I battle with sinus issues. Some of the things I have learned that work better than antibiotics are: Sovereign Silver Nasal Spray, SinuOrega, Eucalyptus and Peppermint essential oils from doTERRA. These are a few of the things that I use to help me get through my sinus episodes. I also use a Neti Pot and it is life-changing!

6. Limit your carb intake. This includes sugar, starches, breads, pasta, etc. These are the things I so love. But guess what? These things don't love us after a while. If we develop healthier eating habits, it will change the course of our lives.

7. **Follow your doctor's orders.** In fact, even if you are on medication, I believe you should keep believing God for healing and keep taking the medication. Every time you take a pill, declare over your body that you are healed and have no need for medicine. Doctors are not evil. They have matriculated through school with a great understanding of the natural workings of the body. However, God created the body. Therefore, He understands the body even more. Seek God for healing, but follow the doctor's orders. You will discover that when you trust God, healing will manifest and the doctors will then take you off your medication.

8. **Free your mind of negative thoughts, feelings and emotions.** When we walk around with anger,

unforgiveness and bitterness, just to name a few, it manifests in our bodies. We must clear our minds of all negativity.

These are just a few suggestions; it is in no way an exhaustive list of what you should do seek a healthy lifestyle. The point of this chapter is to understand that sometimes a person can be sick because he/she are not taking care of themselves. No amount of prayer and fasting can substitute taking care of yourself. It is my prayer that through this book, you will find your healing. Please be encouraged and know that God has your back.

SALVATION

DO YOU KNOW JESUS?

I couldn't let you get to the end of this book and not offer you the opportunity to accept Jesus Christ as your personal Lord and Savior. Having a relationship with Him is one of the most powerful things that have happened to me. We've talked about questioning our faith. I pray that your faith is in such a way that you are now ready to accept what Jesus did on Calvary.

Jesus died on the cross so you could be free from sin. Romans 10:9-10 KJV states, " That if thou shalt confess with thy mouth the Lord Jesus, and shalt believe in thine heart that God hath raised him from the dead, thou shalt be saved. For with the heart man believeth unto righteousness; and with the mouth confession is made unto salvation." Salvation is through Jesus Christ and His work alone. If you are ready to accept Him repeat this prayer:

"Father, I thank you for what Jesus Christ did on Calvary. I receive His gift of salvation today. I ask that you forgive me of all my sins, cleanse me of all unrighteousness and that you would accept me as your child. I confess that

Jesus died on the cross for my sins and that on the third day, He rose again so that I could be free. Thank you for the gift of salvation. In Jesus' name, I pray! Amen."

I know it may seem like you are the same person, but you are now a new creature in Christ. All old things have passed away and behold, all things are new! I want you to know that today, heaven is rejoicing. If you prayed that prayer and you believed it in your heart, I want to be the first to welcome you into the kingdom of God! Your next step is to find a Bible-teaching church where you can learn the Word of God, grow in your faith and fellowship with other believers. Congratulations on making an eternal decision. I'll see you in heaven!

-Apostle Dontez Williams

www.ingramcontent.com/pod-product-compliance
Lightning Source LLC
Chambersburg PA
CBHW071946040426

42447CB00024B/2051